It's Time to Celebrate

CHRISTMAS

Written by
Rebecca Phillips-Bartlett

KidHaven
PUBLISHING

Published in 2026 by
KidHaven Publishing, an Imprint of
Greenhaven Publishing, LLC
2544 Clinton St., Buffalo, NY 14224

Written by: Rebecca Phillips-Bartlett
Edited by: Noah Leatherland
Designed by: Ker Ker Lee

Cataloging-in-Publication Data
Names: Phillips-Bartlett, Rebecca.
Title: Christmas / Rebecca Phillips-Bartlett.
Description: Buffalo, NY : Kidhaven Publishing, 2026. | Series: Its time to celebrate | Includes index and glossary
Identifiers: ISBN 9781534550001 (pbk) | ISBN 9781534550018 (library bound) | ISBN 9781534550025 (ebook)
Subjects: LCSH: Christmas—Juvenile Literature | Holidays—Juvenile Literature
Classification: LCC GT4985.5 P45 2026 | DDC 394.2663 --dc25

Manufactured in the United States of America

CPSIA compliance information: Batch #CSKH26
For further information contact Greenhaven Publishing LLC at 1-844-317-7404.

Please visit our website, www.greenhavenpublishing.com.
For a free color catalog of all our high-quality books, call toll free 1-844-317-7404 or fax 1-844-317-7405.

Find us on

Photo Credits – Images are courtesy of Shutterstock.com. With thanks to Getty Images, Thinkstock Photo, and iStockphoto.

Recurring images –Molesko Studio, KanKhem. Cover – KanKhem, AnastasiiaM, Rolau Elena, Molesko Studio. 2–3 – Tatiana Gordievskaia. 4–5 – Ground Picture, Maria Symchych. 6–7 – Lio putra. 8–9 – 1000 Words, Pixel-Shot. 10–11 – Triteleia. 12–13 – Alones, mikeledray, SeventyFouR. 14–15 –Bogdan Sonjachnyj. 16–17 – CL Medien, Monkey Business Images. 18–19 – OlesyaPogosskaya, Pixel-Shot. 20–21 – David Peperkamp, Lasse Johansson, Teresa Kasprzycka, Tommy Alven. 22–23 – Drazen Zigic, Yuganov Konstantin.

Contents

Words that look like <u>this</u> can be found in the glossary on page 24.

It's Christmas!

Hi! I am Josie. I am counting down the days until the 25th of December. Can you guess why?

The countdown to Christmas is called Advent.

I am counting down to Christmas, of course! It is my favorite time of the year.

Christmas is a Christian festival that honors the birth of Jesus Christ. Christians believe Jesus is the son of God. Many people all over the world celebrate Christmas, even people who are not Christian.

At Christmastime, we put up decorations and eat festive foods.

The Christmas Story

The Christmas story is called the Nativity. This is the Nativity:

Over 2,000 years ago, Mary and Joseph lived in Nazareth. One day, an angel visited Mary. The angel told Mary that she was going to have a baby called Jesus, who would be God's son.

Mary and Joseph traveled to Bethlehem. When they arrived, there was nowhere for them to stay. Luckily, a kind man let them stay in his stable, where Mary gave birth to Jesus.

Jesus was visited by shepherds and wise men who followed a star.

Celebrating Christmas

During Advent, some schools put on a play telling the Nativity story. Many people sing or listen to Christmas songs, such as carols. Carols are religious songs that tell the Christmas story.

Some towns and cities put up lots of lights to celebrate Christmas. Many families decorate their homes with wreaths and Christmas trees. Christmas trees are often decorated with lights and ornaments.

Craft Corner

Let's Make a Christmas Wreath

You will need:

- Scissors
- Green paper or cardstock
- Red paper
- Glue
- Ribbon or string
- A pencil

How to make a wreath:

1. Put your hand on the green paper.
2. Draw around your hand.
3. Cut this hand shape out.

4. Use the green hand as a template to cut out more green hands.
5. Glue the hands together in a circle.
6. Decorate your wreath with red paper.
7. Attach a loop of ribbon to the top of the wreath to hang it up.

Are You Ready for Santa?

Whether you know him as Santa Claus, Father Christmas, or Saint Nicholas, Santa is a much-loved part of Christmas. He spends most of the year in the North Pole making presents with his elves.

On the night before Christmas, many children leave out snacks for Santa.

On *Christmas Eve*, Santa travels around the world in one night in a sleigh pulled by flying reindeer. He squeezes down everyone's chimneys to leave presents in their *stocking*.

Cooking Corner

Let's Bake Gingerbread

You will need:

- 3 tablespoons (44 mL) of molasses
- 1/3 cup (100 g) of brown sugar
- 1/2 cup (100 g) of butter
- 1 3/4 cups (225 g) of all-purpose flour
- 1/2 teaspoon (3 g) of baking soda
- 1 tablespoon (17 g) of cinnamon
- 1 tablespoon (17 g) of ginger
- Cookie cutters
- Parchment paper

How to make gingerbread:

1. Melt the butter in a pan with the molasses and sugar.
2. Mix the remaining ingredients in a bowl.
3. Mix the melted mixture into the dry ingredients to make a dough.
4. Roll the dough until it is 0.2 inches (0.5 cm) thick. Chill in the fridge for one hour.
5. Preheat the oven to 375 degrees Fahrenheit (190 degrees Celsius).
6. Cut shapes into the dough with a cookie cutter.
7. Place the shapes on a lined baking tray. Bake for 10 to 12 minutes.

On Christmas Day

I wake up really early on Christmas morning. I cannot wait to see if Santa has come.

At 9 a.m., my family goes to church. At church, we listen to Bible stories and sing carols.

After church, we cook our Christmas dinner. We have family traveling from far away to join us for dinner, so we make lots of food. After dinner, we play games and watch Christmas movies.

Creative Corner

Let's Write a Christmas Song

Christmas songs are a great way to get into the Christmas spirit. Why not write your own song about what Christmas means to you?

You will need:

- Paper
- A pen or pencil

How to write a Christmas song:

1. Think about your favorite things about Christmas. Write them down.
2. Try writing your song like a poem. Will it rhyme?
3. Think of a tune. Sing your song a few different ways until you find a tune you like.

Christmas Around the World

Many countries all over the world have their own Christmas traditions.

The most famous Christmas decoration in Sweden is the Yule Goat. The Yule Goat is a giant straw goat which is built every December.

Many Swedish families decorate their gardens and Christmas trees with goats.

On Christmas Eve in Poland, many families do not eat dinner until the first star appears in the sky.

Children in Iceland leave a shoe out for the 13 nights before Christmas. The Yule Lads visit overnight and leave presents for good children.

It's Time to Celebrate Christmas

Now you know what Christmas is all about and how people celebrate all over the world. There is only one thing left to do. It is time to celebrate Christmas!

Does your family have any Christmas traditions? Perhaps there is a movie you love to watch together, or a certain snack you always leave out for Santa and his reindeer.

Glossary

Christmas Eve	the day before Christmas
church	a Christian place of worship
festive	to do with a festival, mostly Christmas
play	a story or show that is performed by actors
rhyme	when words end with similar sounds, such as cat and hat
stable	a building built for animals to live in
stocking	a large sock that many children leave out on Christmas Eve for Santa to leave presents in
template	a piece of material used as an outline to create more of the same thing
traditions	beliefs and actions that are passed down between people over time
tune	the pattern of sounds that make up a song

Index